AUDIO ACCESS INCLUDED

SINGER'S EDITION

Disney Princess Songbook

Includes 8 Songs With Warm-Ups and Vocal Instruction

To access audio visit:
www.halleonard.com/mylibrary

Enter Code
1220-6982-5831-2770

ISBN 978-1-4950-5324-5

Walt Disney Music Company
Wonderland Music Company, Inc.

Distributed By

7777 W. Bluemound Rd. P.O. Box 13819 Milwaukee, WI 53213

Disney characters and artwork © Disney Enterprises, Inc.

In Australia Contact:
Hal Leonard Australia Pty. Ltd.
4 Lentara Court
Cheltenham, Victoria, 3192 Australia
Email: ausadmin@halleonard.com.au

For all works contained herein:
Unauthorized copying, arranging, adapting, recording, Internet posting, public performance, or other distribution of the printed or recorded music in this publication is an infringement of copyright. Infringers are liable under the law.

Visit Hal Leonard Online at
www.halleonard.com

Text by Danielle Aldach

Vocals: Sarah Richardson

Piano: J. Mark Baker

Recording Engineer: Ric Probst

The vocal warm-up tracks feature a demonstration of the exercise, then two repetitions by the piano. Listen the first time, then sing along with the piano.

4 Almost There

12 A Dream Is a Wish Your Heart Makes

18 I Wonder

22 Part of Your World

30 Reflection

34 Something There

39 When Will My Life Begin?

44 Where Do I Go from Here

Almost There

The Princess and the Frog

Tiana

Head down to New Orleans for a lesson with Tiana. She is the best princess to teach you breath support. **Breath support** is a vocal technique used to sustain a healthy sound for a long period of time when singing. This first exercise will help you to use your diaphragm. The diaphragm is a flat dome-shaped muscle located just below your lungs. It plays an important role in breathing. Place one hand on your stomach, and feel it expand as you inhale. You should feel it push downward and out just a little with each consonant. In the second exercise, use part of Tiana's song to the evening star to practice taking a nice full breath before singing.

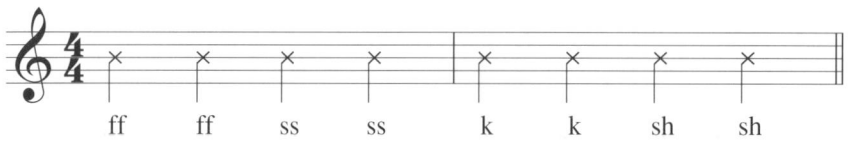

Almost There

from Walt Disney's THE PRINCESS AND THE FROG

Music and Lyrics by
Randy Newman

© 2009 Walt Disney Music Company
All Rights Reserved. Used by Permission.

13
accel.
I know ex - act - ly where I'm go - in'. I'm get - tin' clos - er and clos - er
3
accel.

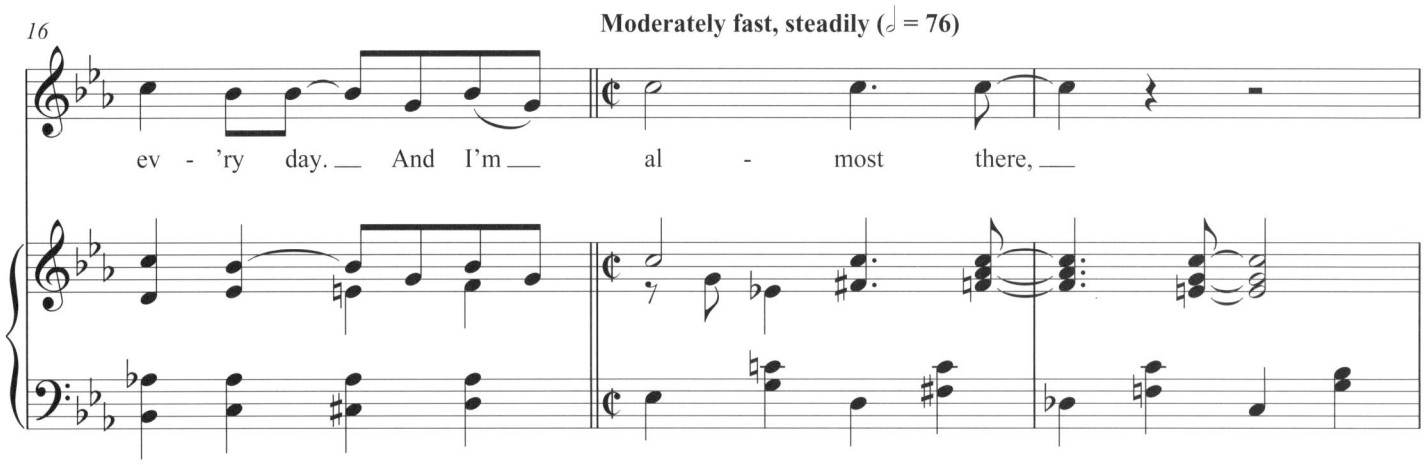
16
Moderately fast, steadily (𝅗𝅥 = 76)
ev - 'ry day. And I'm al - most there,

19
I'm al - most there. Peo - ple down here think I'm

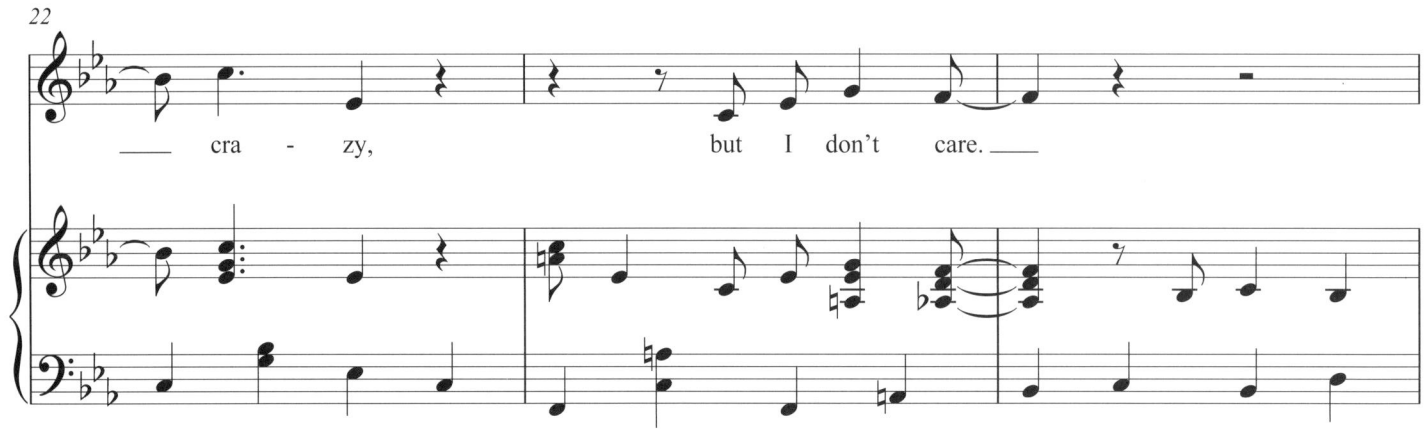
22
cra - zy, but I don't care.

25
Trials and trib - u - la - tions, I've had my share.
28
There ain't noth - ing gon - na stop me now 'cause I'm
31
al - most there.
34
I re - mem - ber Dad - dy told

37
me fair - y tales can come true,
40
but you got - ta make 'em hap - pen; it all de - pends on you.
43
So I work real hard each and ev - 'ry day. Now
46
things for sure are go - ing my way. Just do - ing

49
what I do, look out, boys, I'm com - in' through. And I'm
52
al - most there, I'm al - most there.
55
Peo - ple gon - na come here from ev - 'ry - where, and I'm
58
al - most there, I'm al - most there.

61
65
69
Slower (𝅗𝅥 = c. 104)
There've been trials and trib - u - la - tions. You know I've ___ had ___ my
72
(𝅗𝅥 = 76)
a tempo
share. But I've climbed a moun - tain, I've crossed a riv - ver, and I'm
a tempo

75
al - most there.
I'm al - most there.
78
I'm al - most there.
82
86

A Dream Is a Wish Your Heart Makes

Cinderella

Cinderella

We find Cinderella in the ballroom to practice singing chromatic notes. A musical scale is made up of 12 notes, each a half step apart. **Chromatic** notes are those that do not appear in the key. In a piece of music, these are also referred to as **accidentals**. First, let's practice descending and ascending chromatics. In the second exercise, use part of Cinderella's theme to practice accurate pitches. Use a piano or the recording to listen first, then sing along.

A Dream Is a Wish Your Heart Makes

from Walt Disney's CINDERELLA

Words and Music by Mack David,
Al Hoffman and Jerry Livingston

© 1948 Walt Disney Music Company
Copyright Renewed
All Rights Reserved. Used by Permission.

15
heart - aches: what - ev - er you wish for, you
19
keep. Have faith in your dreams, and some day
24
your rain - bow will come smil - ing through. No mat - ter
29
how your heart is griev - ing, if you keep on be - liev - ing, the dream

34
that you wish will come true.
39
cresc. poco a poco
43
accel.
47
Slightly faster (𝅗𝅥. = c. 52)
mf
A dream is a wish your
ff
mf

51
heart makes when you're fast a - sleep.
3
56
In dreams you will lose your heart - aches: what -
61
ev - er you wish for, you keep. Have
65
faith in your dreams, and some day your

69
rall.
espress.
rain - bow will come smil - ing through.
No mat - ter
rall.
espress.
73
mp
how your heart is griev - ing, if you keep on be - liev - ing, the
mp
77
a tempo
rit.
Slowly, expressively
dream that you wish will come true.
a tempo
rit.
p
82
rit. al fine

I Wonder

Sleeping Beauty

Aurora

Let's go for a walk in the woods with Aurora for a lesson in intervals. An **interval** is the distance between two notes. This distance can be large or small. In the first exercise, we will practice small intervals. In the second exercise, we will practice large intervals. Use a piano or the recording to listen first, then sing along.

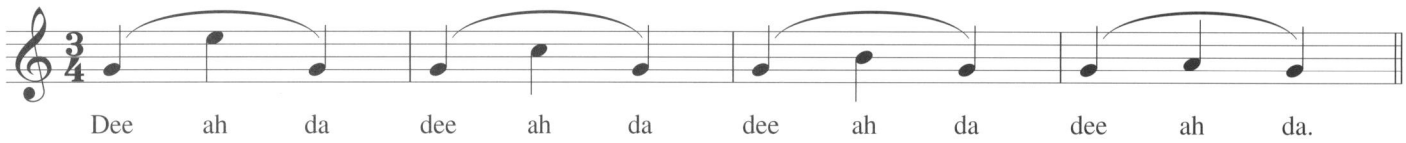

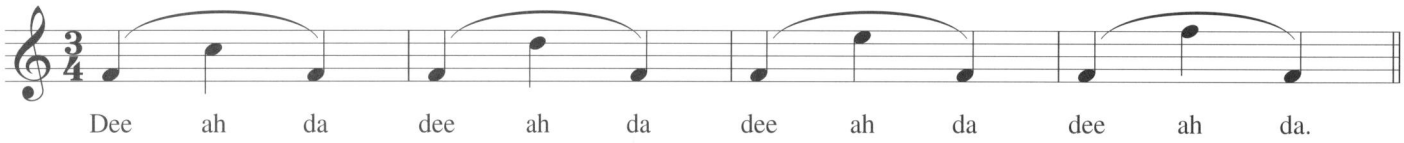

I Wonder

from Walt Disney's SLEEPING BEAUTY

Words by Winston Hibler and Ted Sears
Music by George Bruns
Adapted from a Theme by Tchaikovsky

© 1954 Walt Disney Music Company
Copyright Renewed
All Rights Reserved. Used by Permission.

* For a shorter version, begin here.

37
A gay lit - tle love mel - o - dy? I
42
won - der, I won - der If my heart keeps
47
sing - ing, will my song go wing - ing to some - one Who'll
52
rit.
ten.
find me And bring back a love song to me?
ten.
rit.

Part of Your World

The Little Mermaid

Ariel

Go for a swim in the sea with Ariel to practice singing legato. **Legato** is the Italian word for smooth. Notes in succession should be sung in one connected breath with no space in between. Use Ariel's theme, first ascending, and then descending, to practice singing smoothly.

Part of Your World

from Walt Disney's THE LITTLE MERMAID

Music by Alan Menken
Lyrics by Howard Ashman

© 1988 Wonderland Music Company, Inc. and Walt Disney Music Company
All Rights Reserved. Used by Permission.

13
Look at this trove, treas-ures un - told. How man - y won - ders can
16
one cav - ern hold? Look-ing a - round here you'd think, sure, she's got
19
ev - 'ry - thing. I've got gad - gets and giz - mos a -
22
plen - ty. I've got who - zits and what - zits ga - lore. You want

25
rall.
thing - a - ma- bobs, I've got twen - ty. But who cares? No big
rall.
28
a tempo
rit.
a tempo
deal. I want more. I wan - na be ___ where the
a tempo
rit.
a tempo
32
peo - ple are. I wan - na see, ___ wan - na see 'em danc - in',
35
walk - in' a - round _ on those, what - d' - ya call ___ 'em, oh, feet.

38
Flip - pin' your fins you don't get too far.
41
Legs are re - quired for jump - in', danc - in'. Stroll - in' a - long down the,
3
44
what's that word a - gain, street? Up where they walk, up where they
48
run, up where they stay all day in the sun. Wan - der - in'
rall.
rall.

51
a tempo
free, wish I could be part of that world. What would I
a tempo
55
give if I could live out - ta these wa - ters? What would I
59
pay to spend a day warm on the sand? Bet - cha on
63
land they un - der - stand. Bet they don't re - pri - mand their daugh -

66
rall.
- ters. Bright young wom - en, sick of swim - min', read - y to
rall.
69
a tempo
stand. And read - y to know what the
a tempo
72
peo - ple know. Ask 'em my ques - tions and get some an - swers.
75
What's a fire, and why does it, what's the word, burn?

78
When's it my turn? Would-n't I love, love to ex - plore that shore up a -
82
slower
bove, out of the sea. Wish I could
rit.
slower
86
a tempo
be part of that world.
a tempo
90
rit.

Reflection

Mulan

Mulan

Time to practice in the training fields with Mulan. Here we will learn to sing using dynamics. **Dynamics** are indications of the levels of sound, loud or soft, in a piece of music. In this first exercise, practice singing one whole note at a time. Begin softly, grow louder, and then come back down to soft. In the second exercise, use the dynamics given throughout the melody.

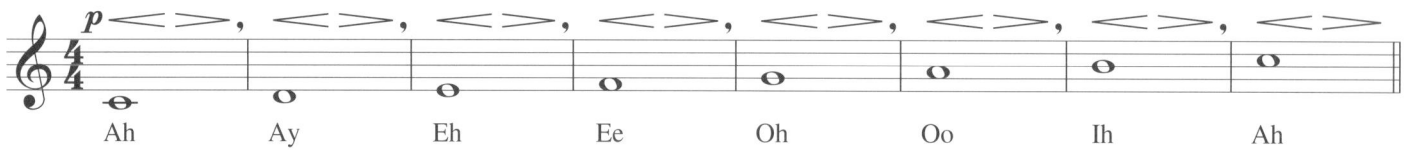

Reflection

from Walt Disney Pictures' MULAN

Music by Matthew Wilder
Lyrics by David Zippel

© 1998 Walt Disney Music Company
All Rights Reserved. Used by Permission.

14
be my-self, I would break my fam - 'ly's heart.
17
mf
Who is that girl I see
mf
20
star - ing straight back at me? Why is my re - flec - tion some - one
f
f
24
I don't know? Some - how I

27
can - not hide who I am, though I've tried.
30
When will my re - flec - tion show who I am in -
33
Slower
mp
rall.
- side? When will my re - flec - tion show who I am in -
f
mp
rall.
37
a tempo
side?
a tempo
rit.

Something There

Beauty and the Beast

Belle

Belle is on the staircase with the Beast practicing arpeggios. **Arpeggios** are the tones of a chord played in succession. In the next two exercises, make sure each note is sung on pitch – and remember to sing legato!

Something There

from Walt Disney's BEAUTY AND THE BEAST

Music by Alan Menken
Lyrics by Howard Ashman

© 1991 Walt Disney Music Company and Wonderland Music Company, Inc.
All Rights Reserved. Used by Permission.

11
why I did - n't see it there be - fore.
cresc.
14
mf
New, and a bit a - larm - ing.
mf
17
Who'd have ev - er thought that this could
20
be?
poco rit.
f a tempo
True
cresc.
poco rit.
f a tempo

23
that he's no Prince Charm - ing, but there's some - thing
26
in him that I sim - ply did - n't see.
ritenuto
29
mp
Well, who'd have thought? Well, who'd have
dim.
mp
a tempo
31
known? And who'd have guessed we'd come to - geth - er on our

33
own? Wait and see... a few days more. There may be
36
some-thing there that was-n't there be - fore. There may be
39
some-thing there that was-n't there be - fore.
42
rit.

When Will My Life Begin?

Tangled

Rapunzel

Rapunzel is the best teacher for rhythm. Rhythm is how notes are counted – long and short lengths. The next two exercises are from Rapunzel's song. Clap and speak each rhythm to practice for "When Will My Life Begin." Use the audio recording if you need to.

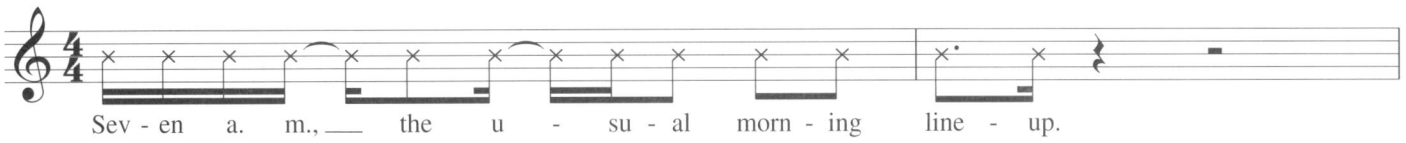

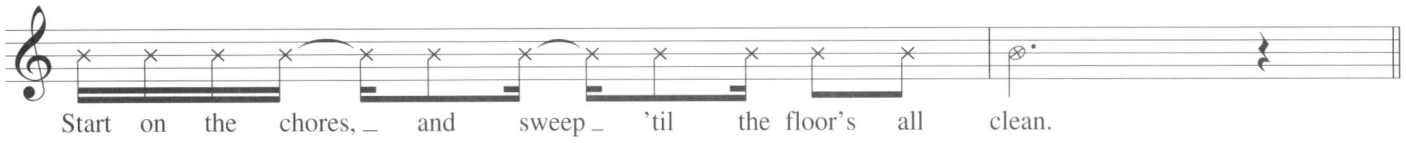

When Will My Life Begin?

from Walt Disney Pictures' TANGLED

Music by Alan Menken
Lyrics by Glenn Slater

© 2010 Wonderland Music Company, Inc. and Walt Disney Music Company
All Rights Reserved. Used by Permission.

9
gain, and by then it's, like, sev - en fif - teen. And so I'll
stretch, may - be sketch, take a climb, sew a dress. And I'll re -
11
read a book, or may - be two or three; I'll add a
read the books if I have time to spare. I'll paint the
13
few more paint - ings to my gal - ler - y; I'll play gui -
walls some more; I'm sure there's room some - where. And then I'll
15
tar, and knit, and cook, and ba - sic - 'ly just won - der,
brush, and brush and brush, and brush my hair, stuck in the

17
1
"When will my life be - gin?"
20
23
2
same place I've al - ways been, and I'll keep won - d'ring and won - d'ring and
26
won - d'ring and won - d'ring, "When will my life be - gin?"
rit.

29
Slowly, freely
mp
To-mor - row night... the lights will ap - pear,
mp
33
just like they do on my birth - day each year.
37
What is it like out there where they glow?
41
rit.
3
Now that I'm old - er, moth-er might just let me go...
3
rit.

Where Do I Go from Here

Pocahontas II: Journey to the New World

Pocahontas

Pocahontas will help you learn phrasing. A **phrase** in music is a complete thought. Think of it like a sentence. The singer expresses the rise and fall of the notes in a complete musical sentence. In the first exercise, use the theme from Pocahontas to apply this musical concept. In the second exercise, practice using the theme from "Where Do I Go from Here" to prepare for the whole song.

Where Do I Go from Here

from Walt Disney's POCAHONTAS II: JOURNEY TO A NEW WORLD

Music by Larry Grossman
Words by Marty Panzer

© 1998 Wonderland Music Company, Inc.
All Rights Reserved. Used by Permission.

10
they sur - vive. When snow's so deep, the bears all sleep to
hard to see, it winds and bends, but where it ends de -
13
keep them - selves a - live. They do what they
pends on on - ly me. In my heart I
3
3
16
must for now and trust in their plan.
don't feel part of so much I've known.
19
If I trust in mine, some - how I might find
Now it seems it's time to start a new life

22
cresc.
who I am.
on my own.
But where
cresc.
mf
26
do I go from here?
So man - y voic - es
30
ring - ing in my ear.
Which is the voice that
34
I was meant to hear?
How will I know?

38
1
Where do I go from here?
42
2
My Where do I
46
f
mp
Slowly
go from here?
f
mp
50
dim. e rit.
pp